BY JON MEACHAM

Thomas Jefferson: The Art of Power

BY ANNETTE GORDON-REED

The Hemingses of Monticello: An American Family

Thomas Jefferson and Sally Hemings:
An American Controversy

In the Hands of the People

AFTERWORD BY
ANNETTE GORDON-REED

JOHN A. RAGOSTA
ASSOCIATE EDITOR

A PROJECT OF THE
THOMAS JEFFERSON FOUNDATION
AT MONTICELLO

RANDOM HOUSE NEW YORK

In the Hands of the People

THOMAS JEFFERSON ON
EQUALITY, FAITH, FREEDOM,
COMPROMISE, AND THE ART
OF CITIZENSHIP

EDITED AND WITH
AN INTRODUCTION BY
JON MEACHAM

Published in the United States by Random House,
an imprint and division of
Penguin Random House LLC, New York.

RANDOM HOUSE and the HOUSE colophon are
registered trademarks of Penguin Random House LLC.

Hardback ISBN 9780593229316
Ebook ISBN 9780593229323

Printed in the United States of America on acid-free paper

randomhousebooks.com

2 4 6 8 9 7 5 3 1

FIRST EDITION

Title-page photograph: interior of dome of
the Jefferson Memorial, © iStock/Douglas Rissing

Book design by Carole Lowenstein

Contents

Introduction

TO ENLIGHTEN THE PEOPLE

Every government degenerates when
trusted to the rulers of the people alone.
The people themselves are its only safe depositories.
—THOMAS JEFFERSON

John Adams was, as usual, skeptical to the point of gloominess. In the long winter of his life, the diminutive, stubborn, and intensely patriotic former president wondered aloud about the vagaries of history, openly worrying that posterity could never fully capture the true story of the birth of the United States. "Who shall write the history of the American Revolution?" Adams wrote to Thomas Jefferson in the summer of 1815, a year shy of the fortieth anniversary of the Declaration of Independence. "Who can write it? Who will ever be able to write it?"

Adams's anxiety was well founded, for he knew that detail and nuance tended to fall victim to the ravages of time and to the narrative need for a beginning, middle, and end of a common story. There is only so much room on a stage, which is among the reasons why heroes are generally singular figures. Even supporting roles are few and far between. Such, Adams believed, would be the fate, and the casting, of the story of America. "The history of our Revolution will be one continued lie from one end to the other," Adams had lamented in a letter to his friend Benjamin Rush as early as 1790, when Adams was serving as the first vice president of the United States. "The essence of the whole will be *that Dr. Franklin's electrical rod smote the Earth and out sprung General Washington. That Franklin electrified him with his rod—and thence forward these two conducted all the policy, negotiations, legislation, and war.*"

Jefferson was characteristically more sanguine than Adams. "I like the dreams of the future," Jefferson once remarked, "better than the history of the past." Adams and Jefferson's exchange about history came as they restored their friendship after the politics of the 1790s had driven them apart. "A letter from you calls up recollections very dear to my mind," Jefferson wrote Adams on Tuesday, January 21, 1812, in reply to an initial note. "It carries me back to the times when, beset with difficulties and dangers, we were fellow laborers in the same cause, struggling for what is most valuable to man, his right of self-government. Laboring always at the same oar, with some wave ever ahead threatening to overwhelm us and yet passing harmless under our bark we knew not how, we rode through the storm with heart and hand, and made a happy port."

It had been a close-run thing, and Jefferson shared

Adams's doubt that subsequent generations would be able to appreciate the tumult and the tension of the war for independence. "On the subject of the history of the American Revolution," Jefferson replied to Adams, "you ask Who shall write it? who can write it? and who ever will be able to write it? Nobody; except merely its external facts. All its councils, designs and discussions, having been conducted by Congress with closed doors, and no member, as far as I know, having even made notes of them. These, which are the life and soul of history, must forever be unknown."

What could be known, however, were the broad lessons of the cataclysmic events of the American Revolution. To Jefferson the details of the struggle against Great Britain were less significant than its meaning—a meaning captured in the words he wrote in the last days of June 1776: "We hold these truths to be self-evident, that all men are created equal, that they are endowed by their Creator with certain unalienable rights, that among these are life, liberty and the pursuit of happiness [and] that to secure these rights, governments are instituted among men, deriving their just powers from the consent of the governed."

The consent of the governed: How, exactly, would the consent of the people—the essence of free government—be formed, expressed, understood, manifested? In Jefferson's mind, the workings of the engine of liberty rested with the people. The art of citizenship depended on the extent to which the people could be relied upon to use experience and reason to move the nation forward through the vagaries of time and chance.

"History," he wrote in his *Notes on the State of Virginia,* "by apprising [the people] of the past, will enable them to judge of the future; it will avail them of the experience of other times and other nations; it will qualify them as judges of the actions and designs of men; it will enable them to know ambition under every guise it may assume; and knowing it, to defeat its views." The fate of freedom—the fate of everything—lay, Jefferson believed, in the broad populace.

His vision was one of hope. "Wherever the people are well informed," Jefferson wrote in 1789, "they can be trusted with their own government, [and] whenever things get so far wrong as to attract their notice, they may be relied on to set them to rights."

Which brings us to the book you are reading now. In an hour of twenty-first-century division and partisanship, of declining trust in institutions and of widespread skepticism about the long-term viability of the American experiment, it is instructive to return to first principles. Not, to be sure, as an exercise in nostalgia or as a flight from the realities of our own time, but as an honest effort to see, as Jefferson wrote, what history may be able to tell us about the role of the people in the present and the future.

And by *us,* I do mean *us.* This project, undertaken by the Thomas Jefferson Foundation, is less about Jefferson and his complexities and more about the American people and *our* complexities. Leadership—the ways and means of the few who hold positions of elected power—tends to dominate our national conversation and consume our national energy. The point of this book, though, and of the conversations it aims to inspire, is to explore citizenship and the role of the people—the ways and means of how we can form dispositions of heart and mind that find expression in the public life of our nation.

Why turn to the slave-owning Thomas Jefferson for counsel on how to live in the diverse world of a global age? The author of the Declaration of Independence and of the Virginia Statute for Religious Freedom was a patriarchal white supremacist; the third president of the United States and the founder of the University of Virginia had little interest in securing the rights of women and played a critical role in the dispossession of native peoples from their lands.

And yet, and yet—so much of our history can be summed up in the phrase "and yet." For all his faults, Jefferson repays our attention. "I have said that the Declaration of Independence is the ringbolt to the chain of your nation's destiny; so, indeed, I regard it," Frederick Douglass said in 1852. "The principles contained in that instrument are saving principles. Stand by those principles, be true to them on all occasions, in all places, against all foes, and at whatever cost."

More than a century later, Martin Luther King, Jr., observed, "The Declaration of Independence proclaimed to a world, organized politically and spiritually around the concept of the inequality of man, that the dignity of human personality was inherent in man as a living being. The Emancipation Proclamation was the offspring of the Declaration of Independence. It was a constructive use of the force of law to uproot a social order which sought to separate liberty from a segment of humanity."

And a quarter of a century after that, at the University of Virginia, Ronald Reagan said of Jefferson, "He knew how disorderly a place the world could be. Indeed, as a leader of a rebellion, he was himself an architect, if you will, of disorder. But he also believed that man had received from God a precious gift of enlightenment—the gift of reason, a gift that could extract from the chaos of life meaning, truth, order."

In many respects Thomas Jefferson *is* America. In his lifetime he spoke of important things, thought widely and deeply about universal issues that shape us still, and fought to bring Enlightenment values to bear on a fallen and unruly reality. And in death he can now serve as inspiration, as warning, and as guide.

. . .

In the summer of 1826, Jefferson's granddaughter Ellen Wayles Coolidge was en route from Boston to Charlottesville when the news of the great man's death reached her in New York. She arrived at Monticello long after the funeral was over. To her, the place that had been his home for so long now seemed a foreign land. "He was gone," she wrote the biographer Henry Randall many years later, recalling the pain of her return. "His place was empty. I visited his grave, but the whole house at Monticello, with its large apartments and lofty ceilings, appeared to me one vast monument."

Such was the power of Jefferson, though, that Ellen expected him to appear to her at any moment—to hear his voice, to look into his eyes, to feel his touch once more. "I wandered about the vacant rooms as if I were looking for him," she wrote.

> Had I not seen him there all the best years of my life? . . . I passed hours in his chamber. It was just as he had left it. There was the bed on which he had slept for so many years—the chair in which, when I entered the room, I ~~had~~ always found him sitting— articles of dress still in their places—his clock by which he had told so many useful hours—In the cabinet adjoining were his books, the beloved companions of his leisure—his writing table from which I gathered some small relics, memoranda and scraps of written paper which I still preserve. All

seemed as if he had just quitted the rooms and there were moments when I felt as if I expected his return.

She was in a curiously dreamlike state. "For days," she wrote, "I started at what seemed the sound of his step or his voice, and caught myself listening for both." Finally she left the house, and the estate, never to return. Her grandfather lived, for her, in her heart and mind.

And in the heart and mind of her nation. Like his grieving granddaughter in the summer of 1826, many Americans have never quite let Jefferson go. "If America is right," the biographer James Parton wrote in 1874, "then Jefferson is right. If America is wrong, then Jefferson is wrong."

It's a remarkable burden to put on any one man or any one vision of politics, but the observation resonates not least because Jefferson represents the best of us and the worst of us. He benefited from a cruel system of human chattel while offering the promise of equality that would, in the fullness of time, find expression in the Thirteenth, Fourteenth, Fifteenth, and Nineteenth amendments to the Constitution, amendments that belatedly extended the meaning of his words to African Americans and to women.

Jefferson's circumstances were particular, yet the general issues that consumed him are constant: liberty and power, rights and responsibilities, the keeping of peace and the waging of war. He was a politician, a public man, in a nation in which politics and public life became—and remain—central. "Man . . . feels that he is a participator in the government of affairs not merely at an election, one day in the year, but every day," Jefferson wrote.

No matter the headlines (or tweets) of the day, the story of the American republic has proven Jefferson right again and again. Although, like all mortals, he was a creature of his time and of his place, Jefferson wrote words that speak to us still, all these years distant. Circumstances change, but some features of life endure from generation to generation.

"The care of human life and happiness, and not their destruction, is the first and only legitimate object of good government," Jefferson wrote in 1809—true then, and true now. He worried about corruption, about appetite, about ambition. Even before the adoption of the Constitution he fretted about executive power running amok. "It becomes of so much consequence to certain nations to have a friend or a foe at the head of our affairs," Jefferson observed in December 1787, "that they will interfere with money and with arms." And yet he always returned to the efficacy of hope. "I know also that laws and institutions must go hand in hand with the progress of the human mind," Jefferson wrote in 1816. "As that becomes more developed, more enlightened, as new discoveries are made, new truths disclosed, and manners and opinions change with the change of circumstances, institutions must advance also, and keep pace with the times."

The collection of Jefferson quotations gathered here is a way to bring the discoveries of old into the debates of a new (or newish) century. They are offered in suggested categories that address perennial democratic phenomena. From the role of reason to the perils of reflexive partisanship to the promise of equality to the centrality of free inquiry and vigorous criticism, these thoughts shed light in a world too often given to generating heat. "Enlighten the people generally," Jefferson wrote, "and tyranny and oppressions of body and mind will vanish like evil spirits at the dawn of day." Taken together, these Jeffersonian observations—including observations about Jefferson from other vantage points—form a kind of manual for citizenship.

This book is not a partisan document. The points expressed in these pages are not about converting Republicans into Democrats or Democrats into Republicans. Far from it: They are about how reasonable people devoted to the American experiment can negotiate an ethos shaped by party feeling. Jefferson knew well that such partisan sentiments would be an eternal feature of a free government. "In every country where man is free to think and to speak, differences of opinion will arise from difference of perception, and the imperfection of reason," he observed while president. "But these differences, when permitted, as in this happy country, to purify themselves by free discussion, are but as passing clouds overshadowing our land transiently, and leaving our horizon more bright and serene."

Or so we may hope. As Jefferson wrote in 1803, "I see too many proofs of the imperfection of human reason to entertain wonder or intolerance at any difference of opinion on any subject; and acquiesce in that difference as easily as on a difference of feature or form: experience having taught me the reasonableness of mutual sacrifices of opinion among those who are to act together, for any common object, and the expediency of doing what good we can, when we cannot do all we would wish."

There is no simple formula for good government, no sure and certain prescription for sound leadership or wise citizenship. We are forever becoming, forever living in tension between the ideal and the real. Great leaps forward are possible; dizzying falls backward are an eternal risk. The best we can do is engage in the arena of public life, always remembering that America is at its best, in the words of Dr. King, spoken at the

March on Washington in 1963, when the nation lives out "the true meaning of its creed"—the creed most brilliantly articulated by Jefferson. We celebrate eras in which we open our arms, not ones in which we clench our fists.

Jefferson can help lead the way. He believed that the republic could survive and thrive only if there were engaged citizens doing the hard work of self-government. Education, attentiveness to public affairs, an openness to new ideas and diverse opinions: Such elements are part of the Jeffersonian infrastructure of informed citizenship. Without citizens armed with information, perspective, and patience, what Jefferson called the "Empire of liberty" might well fail. With such citizens, the future was—and *is*—bright.

Jefferson himself kept the faith. "I will not believe our labors are lost," he wrote John Adams in 1821.

> I shall not die without a hope that light and liberty are on steady advance. . . . The art of printing alone and the vast dissemination of books will maintain the mind where it is, . . . and even should the cloud of barbarism and despotism again obscure the science and liberties of Europe, this country remains to preserve and restore light and liberty to them. In short, the flames kindled on the 4th of July 1776 have spread over too much of the globe to be extinguished by the feeble engines of despotism. On the

contrary they will consume these engines, and all who work them.

That work is now our work. Let us commit our hands and our hearts to the task of keeping those flames alive so that all may one day walk in their light.

In the Hands of the People

THE ONGOING QUEST
FOR EQUALITY

JEFFERSON OFFERED US a bold vision when he declared that all men are created equal. We know that
neither Jefferson, the Founders, nor we fully live up to
that principle, but the standard that Jefferson articulated was inspirational and aspirational. It was a hope
and a promise. It has been used for centuries as a touch-
stone for people seeking freedom and demanding their
own voice in the political process. As Abraham Lincoln
said, Jefferson's words stand as "a rebuke and a stumbling-
block to the very harbingers of reappearing tyranny."
Both the principle of human equality and the continu-
ing struggle for it lie at the foundation of the American
republic, and the finest hours in our history have been
marked by an expansion of those people included in
the Jeffersonian assertion of the summer of 1776.

While Jefferson profited from slavery, America's
tragic original sin, and failed to promote the rights of
all of the members of the American community, he

nonetheless understood that a multi-ethnic nation needed to protect the rights of all of its citizens and actively engage them in its governance. The fundamental principle was adaptable for other people and other times. Human progress would expand its reach. African Americans, women, Native Americans, the LGBTQ communities, and others have, through their own great efforts, put living blood into the heart of the Jeffersonian principle. Jefferson's sight was often narrow—limited to white men—but his vision was broad and powerful, defining much of what is great about America. It has inspired people around the globe and across time, and continues to do so.

> We hold these truths to be self-evident, that all men are created equal, that they are endowed by their Creator with certain unalienable Rights, that among these are Life, Liberty and the pursuit of Happiness. That to secure these rights, Governments are instituted among Men, deriving their just powers from the consent of the governed. . . .
>
> DECLARATION OF INDEPENDENCE*

The equal rights of man and the happiness of every individual are now acknowledged to be the only

---

*In places, Thomas Jefferson's capitalization, punctuation, and spelling have been updated to make this material more accessible to modern readers.

legitimate objects of government. Modern times
have the signal advantage too of having discovered
the only device by which these rights can be
secured, to wit, government by the people acting,
not in person, but by representatives, chosen by
themselves. . . .

THOMAS JEFFERSON TO ADAMANTIOS KORAÏS,
OCTOBER 31, 1823

All too will bear in mind this sacred principle, that
though the will of the majority is in all cases to prevail, that will, to be rightful, must be reasonable;
that the minority possess their equal rights, which
equal laws must protect, and to violate would be
oppression.

THOMAS JEFFERSON'S FIRST INAUGURAL
ADDRESS, MARCH 4, 1801

May it [the Declaration of Independence] be to the
world what I believe it will be, . . . the signal of
arousing men to burst the chains, under which
monkish ignorance and superstition had persuaded
them to bind themselves, and to assume the blessings and security of self-government. . . . All eyes
are opened, or opening to the rights of man. The
general spread of the light of science has already
laid open to every view the palpable truth that the
mass of mankind has not been born, with saddles

on their backs, nor a favored few booted and spurred, ready to ride them legitimately, by the grace of god. These are grounds of hope for others.

THOMAS JEFFERSON TO ROGER CHEW WEIGHTMAN,
JUNE 24, 1826

For let it be agreed that a government is republican in proportion as every member composing it has his equal voice in the direction of its concerns. . . . The true foundation of republican government is the equal right of every citizen in his person, and property, and in their management.

THOMAS JEFFERSON TO SAMUEL KERCHEVAL,
JULY 12, 1816

I will not believe our labors are lost. . . . The art of printing alone and the vast dissemination of books will maintain the mind where it is, . . . and even should the cloud of barbarism and despotism again obscure the science and liberties of Europe, this country remains to preserve and restore light and liberty to them. In short, the flames kindled on the 4th of July 1776 have spread over too much of the globe to be extinguished by the feeble engines of despotism. On the contrary they will consume these engines, and all who work them.

THOMAS JEFFERSON TO JOHN ADAMS,
SEPTEMBER 12, 1821

We hold these truths to be self-evident, that all men are created equal, that they are endowed by their creator with certain inalienable rights, that among these are life, liberty and the pursuit of happiness.

BLACK PANTHERS' TEN-POINT PROGRAM, 1966

And near the beginning of the preamble [of the Declaration] are two simple, soaring sentences that are known to every American. Two sentences that are the very breath of our national life. Two sentences that have come across 221 years with not the slightest loss of power or significance. Two sentences that inspire the world as if they had been written yesterday. We hold these truths to be self-evident, they need no proof or explanation. They are obvious. And they are truths, not assumptions or hypothesis. "All men are created equal," five words, twenty-one letters, a revolutionary thought for the time. Five words that still throw the light of democracy into the darkest corners of tyranny and oppression.

FUTURE SECRETARY OF STATE COLIN POWELL, INDEPENDENCE DAY ADDRESS AT MONTICELLO, JULY 4, 1997

Allow me to say, in conclusion, notwithstanding the dark picture I have this day presented, of the state of the nation, I do not despair of this country. There are forces in operation which must inevitably work the downfall of slavery. "The arm of the Lord is not short-ened," and the doom of slavery is certain. I, therefore, leave off where I began, with hope. While drawing en-couragement from "the Declaration of Independence," the great principles it contains, and the genius of American Institutions, my spirit is also cheered by the obvious tendencies of the age.

FREDERICK DOUGLASS,
"THE MEANING OF JULY 4TH FOR THE NEGRO,"
JULY 5, 1852

But as I continued to think about the matter, I gradu-ally gained a bit of satisfaction from being considered an extremist. . . . Was not Thomas Jefferson an extremist?—"We hold these truths to be self-evident, that all men are created equal." So the question is not whether we will be extremist, but what kind of extrem-ists we will be. Will we be extremists for hate, or will we be extremists for love? Will we be extremists for the preservation of injustice, or will we be extremists for the cause of justice?

MARTIN LUTHER KING, JR.,
"LETTER FROM BIRMINGHAM CITY JAIL,"
APRIL 16, 1963

It was, Virginia, your own Thomas Jefferson that taught me that all men are created equal.

FREDERICK DOUGLASS, JULY 24, 1872

We hold these truths to be self-evident; that all men and women are created equal; that they are endowed by their Creator with certain inalienable rights; that among these are life, liberty, and the pursuit of happiness. . . .

> ELIZABETH CADY STANTON, WOMEN'S RIGHTS
> ADVOCATE, DECLARATION OF
> SENTIMENTS, 1848

The Declaration of Independence proclaimed to a world, organized politically and spiritually around the concept of the inequality of man, that the dignity of human personality was inherent in man as a living being. The Emancipation Proclamation was the off-spring of the Declaration of Independence. It was a constructive use of the force of law to uproot a social order which sought to separate liberty from a segment of humanity.

> MARTIN LUTHER KING, JR.,
> EMANCIPATION PROCLAMATION
> CENTENNIAL ADDRESS,
> SEPTEMBER 12, 1962

The colored woman feels that woman's cause is one and universal; and that not till the image of God, whether in parian or ebony, is sacred and inviolable; not till race, color, sex, and condition are seen as the accidents, and not the substance of life; not till the universal title of humanity to life, liberty, and the pursuit of happiness is conceded to be inalienable to all; not till then is woman's lesson taught and woman's cause won—not the white woman's, nor the black woman's, not the red woman's, but the cause of every man and of every woman who has writhed silently under a mighty wrong.

ANNA JULIA COOPER, AFRICAN AMERICAN
SCHOLAR AND EDUCATOR,
"WOMEN'S CAUSE IS ONE AND UNIVERSAL," 1893

On the Statue of Liberty it says: "Give me your tired, your poor, your huddled masses yearning to be free." ... In the Declaration of Independence, it is written: "All men are created equal and they are endowed with certain inalienable rights." ... And in our National Anthem, it says: "Oh, say does that Star-Spangled Banner yet wave over the land of the free." For Mr. Briggs and Mrs. Bryant and all the bigots out there: That's what America is. No matter how hard you try, you cannot erase those words from the Declaration of Independence. No matter how hard you try, you cannot chip those words off the base of the Statue of Liberty and no matter how hard you try, you cannot sing "The Star-Spangled Banner" without those words. That's what America is. Love it or leave it.

HARVEY MILK, POLITICIAN AND GAY RIGHTS
ADVOCATE, GAY FREEDOM DAY PARADE, JUNE 1978

Americans understood these rights more than two hundred years ago. . . . We are only now learning to believe that we are entitled to the same rights.

ZDENEK JANICEK, WORKERS' RIGHTS ADVOCATE,
AFTER READING THE DECLARATION OF INDEPEN-
DENCE TO POLISH WORKERS, NOVEMBER 27, 1989

I have said that the Declaration of Independence is the ringbolt to the chain of your nation's destiny; so, indeed, I regard it. The principles contained in that instrument are saving principles. Stand by those principles, be true to them on all occasions, in all places, against all foes, and at whatever cost.

FREDERICK DOUGLASS, "THE MEANING OF JULY 4TH
FOR THE NEGRO," JULY 5, 1852

2

THE RIGHT—
AND RESPONSIBILITY—
TO VOTE

A T THE FOUNDING OF OUR NATION, most states restricted voting to property-owning white males. Jefferson realized that the right of suffrage—the right to vote—must be expanded both as a matter of justice and to ensure that political leaders did not turn against the people in favor of a political and economic elite. If all citizens had the right to vote and could exercise that right freely, the people had the ultimate control of the government, and their involvement would be a critical safeguard against corruption. The United States would be the strongest nation on earth if citizens were invested in their own government's success by a fair and equal representation; "every man, at the call of the law," Jefferson said, "would fly to the standard of the law, and would meet invasions of the public order as his own personal concern." To promote voting rights in Virginia, for example, Jefferson went so far as to propose that every man who could not satisfy the state's restrictive voting requirements be given fifty acres by the government so that he could vote. Voting privileges were for him both an essential right and a responsibility—even though his sense of the scope of the early American electorate was limited.

While the nation's economic wealth was built largely on the backs of enslaved African Americans, it would take a civil war to pass the Fifteenth Amendment (which prohibits voting restrictions based on race) and a century-long struggle to win true access to the ballot box, a struggle that endures. And American women, while playing a central role in the economy, education, and life of the nation, would not be granted the constitutional right to vote in federal elections until 1920. While many of Jefferson's statements must be read in the context of his time, his principles were adaptable for all peoples and all times. He understood the foundational and empowering role of broad suffrage and participation in government, and disenfranchised groups throughout our history have bravely claimed that Jeffersonian legacy. Maintaining the power of that legacy means protecting the voting rights of all.

> I was for extending the right of suffrage (or in
> other words the rights of a citizen) to all who had a
> permanent intention of living in the country. . . .
> Whoever intends to live in a country must wish

that country well, and has a natural right of assist-
ing in the preservation of it. . . . The other point of
equal representation [for equal numbers of people]
I think capital and fundamental.

THOMAS JEFFERSON TO EDMUND PENDLETON,
AUGUST 26, 1776

Should things go wrong at any time, the people will
set them to rights by the peaceable exercise of their
elective rights.

THOMAS JEFFERSON TO WILSON CARY NICHOLAS,
APRIL 13, 1806

The rational and peaceable instrument of reform,
[is] the suffrage of the people.

THOMAS JEFFERSON TO SPENCER ROANE,
SEPTEMBER 6, 1819

The elective franchise, if guarded as the ark of our
safety, will peaceably dissipate all combinations to
subvert a constitution dictated by the wisdom, and
resting on the will of the people. That will is the
only legitimate foundation of any government, and
to protect its free expression should be our first
object.

THOMAS JEFFERSON TO THE CITIZENS OF
COLUMBIA, SOUTH CAROLINA,
MARCH 23, 1801

It is proper you should understand what I deem the essential principles of our government[:] . . . a jealous care of the right of election by the people, a mild and safe corrective of abuses which are lopped by the sword of revolution where peaceable remedies are unprovided. . . .

THOMAS JEFFERSON, FIRST INAUGURAL ADDRESS,
MARCH 4, 1801

The right of Representation in the Legislature, [is] a right inestimable to them [the people], and formidable to tyrants only.

DECLARATION OF INDEPENDENCE, JULY 4, 1776

Experience and reflection have but more and more confirmed me in the particular importance of the equal representation [for equal numbers of people]. . . .

THOMAS JEFFERSON TO SAMUEL KERCHEVAL,
JULY 12, 1816

It has been thought that corruption is restrained by confining the right of suffrage to a few of the wealthier of the people: but it would be more effectually restrained by an extension of that right to such numbers as would bid defiance to the means of corruption.

THOMAS JEFFERSON, *NOTES ON THE STATE OF VIRGINIA*,
QUERY XIV

Had I been here [in Virginia] I should probably have proposed a general suffrage because my opinion has always been in favor of it. Still I find very honest men who, thinking the possession of some property necessary to give due independence of mind, are for restraining the elective franchise to property. I believe we may lessen the danger of buying and selling votes, by making the number of voters too great for any means of purchase. . . .

THOMAS JEFFERSON TO JEREMIAH MOORE,
AUGUST 14, 1800

"That to secure these rights, governments are instituted among men, deriving their just powers from the consent of the governed." No definition of democracy has ever improved upon that sentence.

COLIN POWELL, INDEPENDENCE DAY ADDRESS
AT MONTICELLO, JULY 4, 1997

3

THE VITALITY OF
A FREE PRESS

F OR JEFFERSON, it was essential that citizens exercise their right to vote to protect the nation from aristocrats trying to seize power and run the government for the benefit of the few rather than the many. But, for voting to work—for the republic to work—citizens needed to be informed both of what political leaders were doing and of possible abuses of power. A free press, then, is equally essential for a free nation—even when, as in Jefferson's time, the press is highly partisan. In the early republic, newspapers did not pretend to be objective, nor did they try to be; they unapologetically presented the viewpoints of existing political parties and interests within those parties. (The notion of a more neutral press that seeks to publish news, in the motto of *The New York Times,* "without fear or favor," came later.) While Jefferson suffered under the criticism of the press, as do most public servants, he was clear that rather than an enemy of the people, the free press is the bulwark of the republic.

The basis of our governments being the opinion of the people, the very first object should be to keep that right; and were it left to me to decide whether we should have a government without newspapers, or newspapers without a government, I should not hesitate a moment to prefer the latter. But I should mean that every man should receive those papers and be capable of reading them.

THOMAS JEFFERSON TO EDWARD CARRINGTON,
JANUARY 16, 1787

The functionaries of every government have propensities to command at will the liberty and property of their constituents. There is no safe deposit for these but with the people themselves; nor can they be safe with them without information. Where the press is free and every man able to read, all is safe.

THOMAS JEFFERSON TO CHARLES YANCEY,
JANUARY 6, 1816

Our citizens may be deceived for a while, and have been deceived; but as long as the presses can be protected, we may trust to them for light.

THOMAS JEFFERSON TO ARCHIBALD STUART,
MAY 14, 1799

But the only security of all is in a free press. The force of public opinion cannot be resisted when permitted freely to be expressed. The agitation it produces must be submitted to.

THOMAS JEFFERSON TO THE MARQUIS DE LAFAYETTE,
NOVEMBER 4, 1823

Our liberty depends on the freedom of the press, and that cannot be limited without being lost.

THOMAS JEFFERSON TO JAMES CURRIE,
JANUARY 28, 1786

I have stated that the constitutions of our several states vary more or less in some particulars. But there are certain principles in which all agree, and which all cherish as vitally essential to the protection of the life, liberty, property, and safety of the citizen. . . . 5. Freedom of the press, . . . this formidable Censor of the public functionaries, by arraigning them at the tribunal of public opinion, produces reform peaceably, which must otherwise be done by revolution. It is also the best instrument for enlightening the mind of men, improving him as a rational, moral, and social being.

THOMAS JEFFERSON TO ADAMANTIOS KORAÏS,
OCTOBER 31, 1823

4

FAITH AND FREEDOM

JEFFERSON WAS ADAMANT that a person's religion should have no effect on his or her civil rights and capacities. Not only did this rule protect each person's natural right to believe and worship as she or he felt best, but it also meant that religion would not be used as a device to divide the nation. In America, Jefferson saw the diversity of religions as a great strength; in religion, "divided we stand, united we fall," he told one correspondent. The historic effort of "kings, nobles, and priests" to support each other by declaring and enforcing an official, uniform orthodoxy, choosing one religion over another, came at the expense of the people and had to be stopped. Such combinations of church and state had produced rivers of blood in Europe and had to yield to a strict separation. The "tyranny over the mind of man" encouraged by such church-state arrangements was dangerous in a republic where everyone had to think for him- or herself. Believing that religion was a matter between each man and his god, Jefferson insisted that religion would be safest in private hands. He was equally clear that religion should not be used as an excuse to violate impartial laws adopted by the community for legitimate purposes.

> Our civil rights have no dependence on our religious opinions, any more than our opinions in physics or geometry; . . . therefore the proscribing any citizen as unworthy [of] the public confidence by laying upon him an incapacity of being called to offices of trust and emolument, unless he professes or renounces this or that religious opinion, is depriving him injuriously of those privileges and advantages to which in common with his fellow-citizens he has a natural right. . . .
>
> THOMAS JEFFERSON, STATUTE OF VIRGINIA FOR ESTABLISHING RELIGIOUS FREEDOM

No man shall be compelled to frequent or support any religious worship, place, or ministry whatsoever, . . . nor shall otherwise suffer on account of his religious opinions or belief; but that all men shall be free to profess, and by argument to maintain, their opinion in matters of religion, and that the same shall in no wise diminish, enlarge, or affect their civil capacities.

THOMAS JEFFERSON, STATUTE OF VIRGINIA
FOR ESTABLISHING RELIGIOUS FREEDOM

They [legislators] meant to comprehend, within the mantle of [the Statute for Religious Freedom's] protection, the Jew and the Gentile, the Christian and Mahometan [Muslim], the Hindu, and infidel of every denomination.

THOMAS JEFFERSON, *AUTOBIOGRAPHY,* 1821

Believing with you that religion is a matter which lies solely between Man and his God, that he owes account to none other for his faith or his worship, that the legitimate powers of government reach actions only, and not opinions, I contemplate with sovereign reverence that act of the whole American people which declared that *their* legislature should "make no law respecting an establishment of religion, or prohibiting the free exercise thereof," thus building a wall of separation between Church and State.

THOMAS JEFFERSON TO THE DANBURY
BAPTIST ASSOCIATION, JANUARY 1, 1802

To suffer the civil magistrate to intrude his powers into the field of opinion, and to restrain the profession or propagation of principles on supposition of their ill tendency, is a dangerous fallacy which at once destroys all religious liberty. . . . That it is time enough for the rightful purposes of civil government for its officers to interfere when principles break out into overt acts against peace and good order; and finally, that truth is great and will prevail if left to herself, that she is the proper and sufficient antagonist to error, and has nothing to fear from the conflict, unless by human interposition disarmed of her natural weapons, free argument and debate. . . .

THOMAS JEFFERSON, STATUTE OF VIRGINIA FOR
ESTABLISHING RELIGIOUS FREEDOM

Th: Jefferson returns his thanks to [Doctor] de la Motta for the eloquent discourse on the Consecration of the Synagogue of Savannah which he has been so kind as to send him. It excites in him the gratifying reflection that his own country has been the first to prove to the world two truths, the most salutary to human society, that man can govern himself, and that religious freedom is the most effectual anodyne against religious dissension: the maxim of civil government being reversed in that of religion, where its true form is "divided we stand, united we fall."

THOMAS JEFFERSON TO JACOB DE LA MOTTA,
SEPTEMBER 1, 1820

The genuine fruit of the alliance between Church and State, the tenants of which, finding themselves but too well in their present position, oppose all advances which might unmask their usurpations, and monopolies of honors, wealth and power, and fear every change, as endangering the comforts they now hold.

ROCKFISH GAP REPORT OF THE UNIVERSITY
OF VIRGINIA COMMISSIONERS,
AUGUST 4, 1818*

The legitimate powers of government extend to such acts only as are injurious to others. But it does me no injury for my neighbor to say there are twenty gods, or no god. It neither picks my pocket nor breaks my leg.

THOMAS JEFFERSON,
NOTES ON THE STATE OF VIRGINIA,
QUERY XVII

*The Rockfish Gap Commission—made up of one member from each of Virginia's senatorial districts—was given the task of advising the Virginia General Assembly on the best place to locate the new University of Virginia and providing suggestions on how the university should be structured. The commission's report, largely written by Thomas Jefferson, became a founding document for the University of Virginia and an important statement on the role of public education in a republic, and religion in public education.

I have considered it [religion] as a matter between every man and his maker, in which no other, and far less the public, had a right to intermeddle.

THOMAS JEFFERSON TO RICHARD RUSH,
MAY 31, 1813

We have solved, by fair experiment, the great and interesting question whether freedom of religion is compatible with order in government and obedience to the laws; and we have experienced the quiet as well as the comfort which results from leaving everyone to profess freely and openly those principles of religion which are the inductions of his own reason, and the serious convictions of his own enquiries.

THOMAS JEFFERSON TO VIRGINIA BAPTIST
ASSOCIATIONS OF CHESTERFIELD,
NOVEMBER 21, 1808

Your sect [Judaism] by its sufferings has furnished a remarkable proof of the universal spirit of religious intolerance, inherent in every sect, disclaimed by all while feeble, and practiced by all when in power. Our laws have applied the only antidote to this vice, protecting our religious, as they do our civil rights, by putting all on an equal footing.

THOMAS JEFFERSON TO
MORDECAI M. NOAH,
MAY 28, 1818

I consider the government of the [United States] as interdicted by the Constitution from intermeddling with religious institutions, their doctrines, discipline, or exercises. This results . . . from the provision that no law shall be made respecting the establishment, or free exercise, of religion. . . . Certainly no power to prescribe any religious exercise, or to assume authority in religious discipline, has been delegated to the general government. . . . But it is only proposed that I should *recommend,* not prescribe a day of fasting and prayer. That is, that I should *indirectly* assume to the [United States] an authority over religious exercises which the Constitution has directly precluded them from. It must be meant too that this recommendation is to carry some authority, and to be sanctioned by some penalty on those who disregard it: not indeed of fine and imprisonment but of some degree of proscription perhaps in public opinion. And does the change in the nature of the penalty make the recommendation the less *a law* of conduct for those to whom it is directed? I do not believe it is for the interest of religion to invite the civil magistrate to direct its exercises, its discipline or its doctrines. . . .

THOMAS JEFFERSON TO SAMUEL MILLER,
JANUARY 23, 1808

It behooves every man, who values liberty of conscience for himself, to resist invasions of it in the case of others; or their case may, by change of circumstances, become his own. . . . Questions of faith . . . the laws have left between god and himself.

THOMAS JEFFERSON TO BENJAMIN RUSH, APRIL 21, 1803

Reason and experiment have been indulged, and error has fled before them. It is error alone which needs the support of government. Truth can stand by itself. . . . Difference of opinion is advantageous in religion. The several sects perform the office of a *censor morum* over each other.

THOMAS JEFFERSON, *NOTES ON THE STATE OF VIRGINIA*, QUERY XVII

Free enquiry must be indulged; and how can we wish others to indulge it while we refuse it ourselves.

THOMAS JEFFERSON, *NOTES ON THE STATE OF VIRGINIA*, QUERY XVII

They have made a happy discovery that the way to silence religious disputes is to take no notice of them. Let us too give this experiment fair play and get rid, while we may, of those tyrannical laws [punishing heresy].

THOMAS JEFFERSON, *NOTES ON THE STATE OF VIRGINIA*, QUERY XVII

Fix reason firmly in her seat, and call to her tribunal every fact, every opinion. Question with boldness even the existence of a god; because, if there be one, he must more approve the homage of reason than that of blindfolded fear.

THOMAS JEFFERSON TO PETER CARR,
AUGUST 10, 1787

Every religion consists of moral precepts and of dogmas. In the first they all agree. All forbid us to murder, steal, plunder, bear false witness, etc., and these are the articles necessary for the preservation of order, justice, and happiness in society. In their particular dogmas all differ; no two professing the same. These respect vestments, ceremonies, physical opinions, and metaphysical speculations, totally unconnected with morality, and unimportant to the legitimate objects of society.

THOMAS JEFFERSON TO JAMES FISHBACK
(DRAFT; NOT SENT), SEPTEMBER 27, 1809

In that branch of religion which regards the moralities of life, and the duties of a social being, which teaches us to love our neighbors as ourselves, and to do good to all men, I am sure that you and I do not differ. We probably differ on that which relates to the dogmas of theology, the foundation of all sectarianism, and on which no two sects dream

alike. . . . We should all be of one sect, doers of good
and eschewers of evil.

THOMAS JEFFERSON TO EZRA STILES ELY,
JUNE 25, 1819

According to the ordinary fate of those who attempt to enlighten and reform mankind, he [Jesus]
fell an early victim to the jealousy and combination
of the altar and the throne. . . .

THOMAS JEFFERSON, "DOCTRINES OF JESUS
COMPARED WITH OTHERS," APRIL 21, 1803

They wish it to be believed that he can have no religion who advocates its freedom.

THOMAS JEFFERSON TO JOHN ADAMS, JUNE 13, 1815

Reason and free enquiry are the only effectual agents
against error. Give a loose to them, and they will
support the true religion by bringing every false one
to their tribunal, to the test of their investigation.

THOMAS JEFFERSON, *NOTES ON THE STATE OF VIRGINIA,*
QUERY XVII

We all agree in the obligation of the moral precepts
of Jesus: but we schismatize and lose ourselves in
subtleties about his nature, his conception maculate
or immaculate, whether he was a god or not a god,
whether his votaries are to be initiated by simple
aspersion, by immersion, or without water; whether

his priests must be robed in white, in black, or not robed at all; whether we are to use our own reason, or the reason of others, in the opinions we form, or as to the evidence we are to believe. It is on questions of this, and still less importance, that such oceans of human blood have been spilt, and whole regions of the earth have been desolated by wars and persecutions, in which human ingenuity has been exhausted in inventing new tortures for their brethren. It is time then to become sensible how insoluble these questions are by minds like ours, how unimportant, and how mischievous; and to consign them to the sleep of death, never to be awakened from it. The varieties in the structure and action of the human mind, as in those of the body, are the work of our creator, against which it cannot be a religious duty to erect the standard of uniformity. The practice of morality being necessary for the well-being of society, he has taken care to impress its precepts so indelibly on our hearts, that they shall not be effaced by the whimsies of our brain. Hence we see good men in all religions, and as many in one as another.

THOMAS JEFFERSON TO JAMES FISHBACK
(DRAFT; NOT SENT), SEPTEMBER 27, 1809

[As to] the right of discussing public affairs in the pulpit . . . I admit the right in general conversation, and in writing; . . . but I suppose there is not an instance of a single congregation which has employed their preacher for the mixt purposes of lecturing them from the pulpit, in chemistry, in medicine, in law, in the science and principles of government, or in any thing but religion exclusively. Whenever therefore preachers, instead of a lesson in religion, put them off with a discourse . . . on the construction of government, or the characters or conduct of those administering it, it is a breach of contract, depriving their audience of the kind of service for which they are salaried, and giving them, instead of it, what they did not want, or, if wanted, would rather seek from better sources. . . . I agree too that on all other occasions the preacher has the right, equally with every other citizen, to express his sentiments, in speaking or writing, on the subjects of medicine, law, politics, etc., his leisure time being his own, and his congregation not obliged to listen to his conversation, or to read his writings. . . .

THOMAS JEFFERSON TO PETER H. WENDOVER
(DRAFT; NOT SENT),
MARCH 13, 1815

His [Jefferson's] researches were deep and extensive. And the result of these researches, was conviction of the truth of the [religious] system he adopted, but at the same time of the most perfect tollerance [sic] toward other men's opinions. "I judge every man's faith by his life," said he in a letter to me, "and I wish my fellow citizens to judge of mine by the same test."

MARGARET BAYARD SMITH, EARLY AMERICAN
AUTHOR, TO JANE BAYARD KIRKPATRICK,
MARCH 31, 1830

5

THE ROLE OF EDUCATION

JEFFERSON EXPLAINED that an educated citizenry was essential in a free republic. With a solid understanding of history and political science, educated citizens would protect the nation by recognizing threats to freedom, by intelligently exercising their right to vote, and by demanding sound government. Leaders who would place public interest above self-interest and partisan politics were also needed, and a sound education would help to create such leaders. Education, expanding the horizon of knowledge, would also encourage human progress and enlightenment. In this way, each generation could improve upon the previous generation, and a free, educated nation could be a beacon to the world. Jefferson was one of the first to propose broad, free, basic public education—for boys *and* girls. Given that education of the citizens and of leaders is a crucial foundation for the nation, he saw that taxes for public education would be investments with a bounteous return. Although his proposals in that regard were not adopted in his lifetime, he did become the "father of the University of Virginia," America's first truly secular university.

> Preach, my dear Sir, a crusade against ignorance; establish and improve the law for educating the common people. Let our countrymen know that the people alone can protect us against these evils [ignorance and prejudices], and that the tax which will be paid for this purpose [public education] is not more than the thousandth part of what will be paid to kings, priests and nobles who will rise up among us if we leave the people in ignorance.
>
> THOMAS JEFFERSON TO GEORGE WYTHE,
> AUGUST 13, 1786

> I hope the education of the common people will be attended to; convinced that on their good sense we may rely with the most security for the preservation of a due degree of liberty.
>
> THOMAS JEFFERSON TO JAMES MADISON,
> DECEMBER 20, 1787

> I know no safe depository of the ultimate powers of the society, but the people themselves: And if we think them not enlightened enough to exercise their control with a wholesome discretion, the rem-

edy is not to take it from them but to inform their discretion by education. This is the true corrective of abuses of constitutional power.

THOMAS JEFFERSON TO WILLIAM C. JARVIS,
SEPTEMBER 28, 1820

If the condition of man is to be progressively ame-liorated, as we fondly hope and believe, [education] is to be the chief instrument in effecting it.

THOMAS JEFFERSON TO ELEUTHÈRE IRÉNÉE
DU PONT DE NEMOURS, SEPTEMBER 9, 1817

Our new University [of Virginia] . . . will be based on the illimitable freedom of the human mind. For here we are not afraid to follow truth wherever it may lead, nor to tolerate any error so long as reason is left free to combat it.

THOMAS JEFFERSON TO WILLIAM ROSCOE,
DECEMBER 27, 1820

And whereas it is generally true that people will be happiest whose laws are best, and are best adminis-tered, and that laws will be wisely formed, and hon-estly administered, in proportion as those who form and administer them are wise and honest; whence it becomes expedient for promoting the public happiness that those persons, whom nature hath endowed with genius and virtue, should be rendered by liberal education worthy to receive and able to guard the sacred deposit of the rights and liberties of their fellow citizens, and that they should be called to that charge without regard to wealth, birth or other accidental condition or circumstance. . . .

THOMAS JEFFERSON, A BILL FOR THE MORE
GENERAL DIFFUSION OF KNOWLEDGE

Nor must we omit to mention, among the benefits of education, the incalculable advantage of training up able counsellors to administer the affairs of our country in all its departments, legislative, executive, and judiciary, and to bear their proper share in the councils of our national government; nothing, more than education, advancing the prosperity, the power and the happiness of a nation.

ROCKFISH GAP REPORT OF THE UNIVERSITY OF
VIRGINIA COMMISSIONERS,
AUGUST 4, 1818

I think by far the most important bill in our whole code is that for the diffusion of knowledge among the people. No other sure foundation can be devised for the preservation of freedom, and happiness.

THOMAS JEFFERSON TO GEORGE WYTHE,
AUGUST 13, 1786

It is safer to have a whole people respectably enlightened than a few in a high state of science and
the many in ignorance. This last is the most dangerous state in which a nation can be.

THOMAS JEFFERSON TO JOSEPH C. CABELL,
JANUARY 13, 1823

My hopes [for a state university] however are kept
in check by the ordinary character of our state leg-
islatures, the members of which do not generally
possess information enough to perceive the important truths, that knowledge is power, that knowledge is safety, and that knowledge is happiness.

THOMAS JEFFERSON TO GEORGE TICKNOR,
NOVEMBER 25, 1817

The advantages of well-directed education, moral,
political and economical, are truly above all esti-
mate. Education generates habits of application, of
order and love of virtue, and controls, by the force
of habit, any innate obliquities in our moral organi-
zation.

ROCKFISH GAP REPORT OF THE UNIVERSITY OF
VIRGINIA COMMISSIONERS,
AUGUST 4, 1818

I cannot too much applaud your desire to improve
your mind; as next to an honest man, the enlight-

ened one is most happy within himself, and most valued by others.

THOMAS JEFFERSON TO PETER JEFFERSON ARCHER,
MARCH 10, 1818

We fondly hope that the instruction which may flow from this institution, kindly cherished, by advancing the minds of our youth with the growing science of the times, and elevating the views of our citizens generally to the practice of the social duties, and the functions of self-government, may ensure to our country the reputation, the safety and prosperity, and all the other blessings which experience proves to result from the cultivation and improvement of the general mind. And, without going into the monitory history of the ancient world, in all its quarters, and at all its periods, that of the soil on which we live, and of its occupants, indigenous and immigrant, teaches the awful lesson, that no nation is permitted to live in ignorance with impunity.

UNIVERSITY OF VIRGINIA
BOARD OF VISITORS REPORT,
NOVEMBER 29–30, 1821

A system of general instruction, which shall reach every description of our citizens from the richest to the poorest, as it was the earliest, so will it be the latest, of all the public concerns in which I shall permit myself to take an interest.

THOMAS JEFFERSON TO JOSEPH C. CABELL,
JANUARY 14, 1818

The objects of this primary education determine its character and limits. These objects would be,

To give to every citizen the information he needs for the transaction of his own business. . . .

To understand his duties to his neighbours, and country, and to discharge with competence the functions confided to him by either.

To know his rights; to exercise with order and justice those he retains; to choose with discretion the fiduciaries of those he delegates; and to notice their conduct with diligence, with candor, and judgment. . . .

ROCKFISH GAP REPORT OF THE
UNIVERSITY OF VIRGINIA COMMISSIONERS,
AUGUST 4, 1818

To expound the principles and structure of government, the laws which regulate the intercourse of nations, those formed municipally for our own government, and a sound spirit of legislation, which banishing all arbitrary and unnecessary restraint on individual action shall leave us free to do whatever does not violate the equal rights of another. . . .

To develop the reasoning faculties of our youth, enlarge their minds, cultivate their morals, and instill into them the precepts of virtue and order. . . .

And generally to form them to habits of reflection, and correct action, rendering them examples of virtue to others and of happiness within themselves.

These are the objects of that higher grade of education, the benefits and blessings of which the legislature now propose to provide for the good and ornament of their country: the gratification and happiness of their fellow citizens, of the parent especially, and his progeny on which all his affections are concentrated. . . .

ROCKFISH GAP REPORT OF THE
UNIVERSITY OF VIRGINIA COMMISSIONERS,
AUGUST 4, 1818

It is highly interesting to our country, and it is the duty of its functionaries to provide, that every citizen in it should receive an education proportioned to the condition and pursuits of his life.

THOMAS JEFFERSON TO PETER CARR,
SEPTEMBER 7, 1814

[Jefferson] failed, in a valiant effort, to persuade the General Assembly of Virginia to set up a system of free

public schools, and we are still today paying the price of not having done so.

MILLS E. GODWIN, JR., FORMER GOVERNOR OF THE
COMMONWEALTH OF VIRGINIA, INDEPENDENCE DAY
ADDRESS AT MONTICELLO,
JULY 5, 1971

[Jefferson] said that it was essential that people understand these issues [that power corrupts], be educated, involve themselves in the political process. Without that, he said, the wolves will take over. . . . He argued that the cost of education is trivial compared to the cost of leaving government to the wolves. The people must rule.

CARL SAGAN, PROFESSOR OF ASTRONOMY AND SPACE
SCIENCES, CORNELL UNIVERSITY, INDEPENDENCE
DAY ADDRESS AT MONTICELLO,
JULY 4, 1992

[Jefferson] argued again in 1779 that the foundations of citizenship are founded or laid in common schools, which he described as being important to advance the knowledge and well-being of mankind. He wanted Americans to be educated so that they could protect their own personal freedoms.

JOHN T. CASTEEN III, PRESIDENT, UNIVERSITY OF
VIRGINIA, INDEPENDENCE DAY ADDRESS
AT MONTICELLO, JULY 4, 1993

6

REFLECTIVE PATRIOTISM VERSUS REFLEXIVE PARTISANSHIP

JEFFERSON WAS CLEAR that the rights and benefits of citizenship come also with obligations. He was realistic, too, that partisan feeling was an inevitable, if lamentable, feature of free government. He often engaged in heated political debates, but he never lost sight of the fact that what united the American people was far more important than what divided them. The key challenge for American citizens was to strike a proper balance between the common good and individual appetites; between party loyalties and the public interest; between a general loyalty to the diversity and promise of the American experiment and one's own personal designs.

Jefferson also recognized that America was a diverse nation, with people of many different religions, ethnicities, and cultures, and would be more diverse over time. It was essential, then, that people would engage across those differences to discuss and debate issues of national importance. Doing so could produce new insights and assist the people to work together to solve complex problems. As a result, Jefferson embraced a vigorous but civil public political discourse (refusing only to engage publicly with dogmatic extremists who had no interest in polite discourse, compromise, or a democratic government).

Enlighten the people generally, and tyranny and oppressions of body and mind will vanish like evil spirits at the dawn of day.

THOMAS JEFFERSON TO PIERRE SAMUEL
DU PONT DE NEMOURS, APRIL 24, 1816

Experience hath shewn that even under the best forms [of government] those entrusted with power have, in time, and by slow operations, perverted it into tyranny; and it is believed that the most effectual means of preventing this would be to illuminate, as far as practicable, the minds of the people at large, and more especially to give them knowledge of those facts which history exhibiteth that, possessed thereby of the experience of other ages and countries, they may be enabled to know ambition under all its shapes, and prompt to exert their natural powers to defeat its purposes. . . .

THOMAS JEFFERSON, A BILL FOR THE
MORE GENERAL DIFFUSION OF KNOWLEDGE

If a nation expects to be ignorant and free, in a state of civilization, it expects what never was and never will be.

> THOMAS JEFFERSON TO CHARLES YANCEY,
> JANUARY 6, 1816

Ignorance and despotism seem made for each other.

> THOMAS JEFFERSON TO ROBERT PLEASANTS,
> AUGUST 27, 1796

Wherever the people are well informed they can be trusted with their own government; that whenever things get so far wrong as to attract their notice, they may be relied on to set them to rights.

> THOMAS JEFFERSON TO RICHARD PRICE,
> JANUARY 8, 1789

No one more sincerely wishes the spread of information among mankind than I do, and none has greater confidence in its effect towards supporting free and good government.

> THOMAS JEFFERSON TO THE
> TRUSTEES OF EAST TENNESSEE COLLEGE,
> MAY 6, 1810

It is an axiom in my mind that our liberty can never be safe but in the hands of the people themselves, and that too of the people with a certain degree of instruction. This it is the business of the state to effect, and on a general plan.

THOMAS JEFFERSON TO GEORGE WASHINGTON,
JANUARY 4, 1786

He who receives an idea from me, receives instruction himself, without lessening mine; as he who lights his taper at mine, receives light without darkening me. That ideas should freely spread from one to another over the globe, for the moral and mutual instruction of man and improvement of his condition, seems to have been peculiarly and benevolently designed by nature, when she made them, like fire, expansible over all space without lessening their density in any point; and like the air in which we breathe, move, and have our physical being, incapable of confinement, or exclusive appropriation. Inventions then cannot in nature be a subject of property.

THOMAS JEFFERSON TO ISAAC MCPHERSON,
AUGUST 13, 1813

I believe this, on the contrary, the strongest government on earth. I believe it the only one, where every man, at the call of the laws, would fly to the standard of the law and would meet invasions of the public order as his own personal concern.

THOMAS JEFFERSON, FIRST INAUGURAL ADDRESS,
MARCH 4, 1801

Lethargy [is] the forerunner of death to the public liberty.

THOMAS JEFFERSON TO
WILLIAM STEPHENS SMITH,
NOVEMBER 13, 1787

The influence over government must be shared among all the people. If every individual which composes their mass participates of the ultimate authority, the government will be safe; because the corrupting the whole mass will exceed any private resources of wealth. . . .

THOMAS JEFFERSON, *NOTES ON THE STATE OF VIRGINIA*,
QUERY XIV

A nation united can never be conquered.

THOMAS JEFFERSON TO JOHN ADAMS,
JANUARY 11, 1816

There is a debt of service due from every man to his country, proportioned to the bounties which nature and fortune have measured to him.

THOMAS JEFFERSON TO
EDWARD RUTLEDGE,
DECEMBER 27, 1796

The right of our fellow citizens to represent to the public functionaries their opinion, on proceedings interesting to them, is unquestionably a constitutional right, often useful, sometimes necessary, and will always be respectfully acknowledged by me.

THOMAS JEFFERSON TO NEW HAVEN MERCHANTS,
JULY 12, 1801

It is impossible not to be sensible that we are acting for all mankind: that circumstances denied to others, but indulged to us, have imposed on us the duty of proving what is the degree of freedom and self-government in which a society may venture to leave its individual members.

THOMAS JEFFERSON TO JOSEPH PRIESTLY,
JUNE 19, 1802

The man who loves his country on its own account, and not merely for its trappings of interest or power, can never be divorced from it; can never refuse to come forward when he finds that she is engaged in dangers which he has the means of warding off.

THOMAS JEFFERSON TO ELBRIDGE GERRY,
JUNE 21, 1797

Where every man is a sharer in the direction of his ward-republic [local government], or of some of the higher ones, and feels that he is a participator in the government of affairs not merely at an election, one day in the year, but every day; when there shall

not be a man in the state who will not be a member
of some one of its councils, great or small, he will
let the heart be torn out of his body sooner than
his power be wrested from him by a Caesar or a
Bonaparte.

THOMAS JEFFERSON TO JOSEPH C. CABELL,
FEBRUARY 2, 1816

Perhaps the single thing which may be required to
others before toleration [is granted] to them would
be an oath that they would allow toleration to others.

THOMAS JEFFERSON, "NOTES ON LOCKE
AND SHAFTESBURY," 1776

We have called by different names brethren of the
same principle. We are all republicans: We are all
federalists. If there be any among us who would
wish to dissolve this union, or to change its republican form, let them stand undisturbed as monuments of the safety with which error of opinion
may be tolerated where reason is left free to
combat it.

THOMAS JEFFERSON, FIRST INAUGURAL ADDRESS,
MARCH 4, 1801

Let us then, fellow citizens, unite with one heart
and one mind, let us restore to social intercourse
that harmony and affection without which liberty,
and even life itself, are but dreary things. And let us

reflect that having banished from our land that religious intolerance under which mankind so long bled and suffered, we have yet gained little if we countenance a political intolerance, as despotic, as wicked, and capable of as bitter and bloody persecutions.

THOMAS JEFFERSON, FIRST INAUGURAL ADDRESS, MARCH 4, 1801

In every country where man is free to think and to speak, differences of opinion will arise from difference of perception and the imperfection of reason. But these differences, when permitted, as in this happy country, to purify themselves by free discussion, are but as passing clouds overshadowing our land transiently and leaving our horizon more bright and serene. That love of order and obedience to the laws, which so considerably characterizes the citizens of the United States, are sure pledges of internal tranquility. . . .

THOMAS JEFFERSON TO THE CITIZENS OF COLUMBIA, SOUTH CAROLINA, MARCH 23, 1801

I never considered a difference of opinion in politics, in religion, in philosophy, as cause for withdrawing from a friend.

THOMAS JEFFERSON TO WILLIAM HAMILTON, APRIL 22, 1800

I can with truth reciprocate the assurances that differences of political opinions excited in me no unfriendliness more than a difference of feature. . . . I can say with truth, and with great comfort to my own heart, that I never deserted a friend for differences of opinion in politics, in religion, in physics; for I place all these differences on a footing.

THOMAS JEFFERSON TO HENRY KNOX,
APRIL 8, 1800

Most controversies begin with a discussion of principles; but soon degenerate into episodical, verbal, or personal cavils. Too much of this is seen in these pamphlets, and, as usual, those whose dogmas are the most unintelligible are the most angry.

THOMAS JEFFERSON TO SALMA HALE,
JULY 26, 1818

Men have differed in opinion, and been divided into parties by these opinions, from the first origin of societies; and in all governments where they have been permitted freely to think and to speak. . . . In this way, and in answers to addresses, you and I could indulge ourselves. We have probably done it, sometime[s] with warmth, often with prejudice, but always, as we believed, adhering to truth. . . . To me then it appears that there have been differences of opinion, and party differences, from the first es-

tablishment of governments, to the present day;
and on the same question which now divides our
own country: that these will continue thro' all future time: that every one takes his side in favor of
the many, or of the few, according to his constitution, and the circumstances in which he is placed:
that opinions, which are equally honest on both
sides, should no[t] affect personal esteem, or social
intercourse: . . . and that wisdom and duty dictate
an humble resignation to the verdict of ou[r] future
peers. In doing this myself, I shall certainly not suffer moot question[s] to affect the sentiments of
sincere friendship and respect. . . .

THOMAS JEFFERSON TO JOHN ADAMS, JUNE 27, 1813

*The mind that conceived Monticello's original design
also helped to conceive an approach to government
that had never truly been tried before. It was based on
a conception of the individual not as a mere subject to
the throne, but as a citizen with responsibilities and
rights, and tracing all the powers of government back
to the will and consent of the people.*

MADELEINE K. ALBRIGHT, SECRETARY OF STATE,
INDEPENDENCE DAY ADDRESS AT MONTICELLO,
JULY 4, 2000

*He believed in the primacy of the role of the people. For
Thomas Jefferson, a well-ordered democracy rose like a*

pyramid from like and local communities. He argued that every citizen ought to participate in civil affairs— especially so in the towns and villages where people lived.

JOHN T. CASTEEN III, INDEPENDENCE DAY ADDRESS
AT MONTICELLO, JULY 4, 1993

7

THE ART AND SCIENCE
OF COMPROMISE

M AKING A REPUBLIC WORK means that compromise among people of different views is often
necessary, and a person (even Jefferson) will often find
him- or herself in the minority on an important political question. In those instances, the will of the majority
(if it protects the equal rights of the minority) must be
accepted.

Even in the early republic, America was made up of
citizens with a broad mix of ethnicities, religions, and
national origins; this made compromise particularly important. Jefferson believed not only that compromise
was essential, but that people would be willing to accept
compromises and political decisions with which they did
not agree if they could participate fairly in the political
process and were thus invested in the government.

A government held together by the bands of reason
only, requires much compromise of opinion, that

things even salutary should not be crammed down the throats of dissenting brethren, especially when they may be put into a form to be willingly swallowed, and that a great deal of indulgence is necessary to strengthen habits of harmony and fraternity.

THOMAS JEFFERSON TO EDWARD LIVINGSTON,
APRIL 4, 1824

I see too many proofs of the imperfection of human reason to entertain wonder or intolerance at any difference of opinion on any subject; and acquiesce in that difference as easily as on a difference of feature or form: experience having taught me the reasonableness of mutual sacrifices of opinion among those who are to act together, for any common object, and the expediency of doing what good we can, when we cannot do all we would wish.

THOMAS JEFFERSON TO JOHN RANDOLPH,
DECEMBER 1, 1803

With the same honest views, the most honest men often form different conclusions.

THOMAS JEFFERSON TO ROBERT R. LIVINGSTON,
SEPTEMBER 9, 1801

Difference of opinion leads to enquiry, and enquiry to truth; and that, I am sure, is the ultimate and sincere object of us both. We both value too much

the freedom of opinion sanctioned by our Constitution, not to cherish its exercise even where in op-
position to ourselves.

THOMAS JEFFERSON TO PETER H. WENDOVER
(DRAFT; NOT SENT), MARCH 13, 1815

I . . . perceive you [the General Assembly] have
many matters before you of great moment. I have
no fear but that the legislature will do on all of
them what is wise and just. . . . With the legislature
I cheerfully leave it to apply this medicine, or that
medicine, or no medicine at all. I am sure their in-
tentions are faithful, and embarked in the same
bottom, I am willing to swim or sink with my fellow citizens. If the latter is their choice, I will go
down with them without a murmur. But my exhor-
tation would rather be "not to give up the ship."

THOMAS JEFFERSON TO CHARLES YANCEY,
JANUARY 6, 1816

I agree . . . that a professorship of Theology should
have no place in our [state] institution. But we cannot always do what is absolutely best. Those with
whom we act, entertaining different views, have the
power and the right of carrying them into practice.
Truth advances and error recedes step by step only;
and to do to our fellow-men the most good in our
power, we must lead where we can, follow where we

cannot, and still go with them, watching always the favorable moment for helping them to another step.

THOMAS JEFFERSON TO THOMAS COOPER,
OCTOBER 7, 1814

Laws made by common consent must not be trampled on by individuals.

THOMAS JEFFERSON TO GARRET VAN METER,
APRIL 27, 1781

8

WEALTH AND ITS DISPARITIES

JEFFERSON WAS REMARKABLY PRESCIENT in his understanding of the possible threats to the United States. He understood that a republic will work only if citizens are broadly committed to its success, which means that everyone must share not only in the rights and responsibilities, but also in the benefits and achievements of the nation. When the benefits (economic or political) seem mostly limited to the few, it can destroy a republic through apathy or revolution. Even as the Founders were constructing the new nation, Jefferson was clear that if the wealth gap between rich and poor grew too large, the very survival of the republic requires that the legislature take decisive action.

I am conscious that an equal division of property is impracticable. But the consequences of this enormous inequality producing so much misery to the bulk of mankind, legislators cannot invent too many devices for subdividing property, only taking care to let their subdivisions go hand in hand with the natural affections of the human mind. . . . Another means of silently lessening the inequality of property is to exempt all from taxation below a certain point, and to tax the higher portions of property in geometrical progression as they rise.

THOMAS JEFFERSON TO JAMES MADISON,
OCTOBER 28, 1785

We have no paupers. . . . The great mass of our population is of laborers; our rich, who can live without labor, either manual or professional, being few and of moderate wealth. Most of the laboring class possess property, cultivate their own lands, have families, and from the demand for their labor are enabled to exact from the rich and the competent such prices as enable them to be fed abundantly, clothed above mere decency, to labor moderately and raise their families. . . . The wealthy, on the other hand, and those at their ease, know nothing of what the Europeans call luxury. They have only somewhat more of the comforts and decencies of life than those who furnish them. Can any condition of society be more desirable than this?

THOMAS JEFFERSON TO THOMAS COOPER,
SEPTEMBER 10, 1814

My walk led me into a train of reflections on that unequal division of property which occasions the numberless instances of wretchedness which I had observed in this country [France] and is to be observed all over Europe.

THOMAS JEFFERSON TO JAMES MADISON,
OCTOBER 28, 1785

The earth is given as a common stock for man to labor and live on. If for the encouragement of industry we allow it to be appropriated, we must take care that other employment be furnished to those excluded from the appropriation. If we do not, the fundamental right to labor the earth returns to the unemployed. It is too soon yet in our country to say that every man who cannot find employment but who can find uncultivated land shall be at liberty to cultivate it, paying a moderate rent. But it is not too soon to provide by every possible means that as few as possible shall be without a little portion of land.

THOMAS JEFFERSON TO JAMES MADISON,
OCTOBER 28, 1785

Instead of an aristocracy of wealth, of more harm and danger than benefit to society, to make an opening for the aristocracy of virtue and talent, which nature has wisely provided for the direction of the interests of society and scattered with equal

hand thro' all its conditions, was deemed essential
to a well ordered republic. To effect it no violence
was necessary, no deprivation of natural right, but
rather an enlargement of it by a repeal of the law
[of primogeniture]. For this would authorize the
present holder to divide the property among his
children equally, as his affections were divided; and
would place them by natural generation on the level
of their fellow citizens.

THOMAS JEFFERSON, *AUTOBIOGRAPHY*, 1821

I love to see honest men and honorable men at the
helm, men who will not bend their politics to their
purses, nor pursue measures by which they may
profit, and then profit by their measures. *Au diable les
Bougres!* [To the devil with fools!]

THOMAS JEFFERSON TO EDWARD RUTLEDGE,
DECEMBER 27, 1796

Unless that mass [the people] retains a sufficient
control over those entrusted with the powers of
their government, these will be perverted to their
own oppression and to the perpetuation of wealth
and power in the individuals, and their families, se-
lected for the trust.

THOMAS JEFFERSON TO
FRANCIS ADRIAN VAN DER KEMP,
MARCH 22, 1812

The people of England, I think, are less oppressed than here [France]. But it needs but half an eye to see, when among them, that the foundation is laid in their dispositions for the establishment of a despotism. Nobility, wealth, and pomp are the objects of their adoration. They are by no means the free-minded people we suppose them in America. Their learned men too are few in number, and are less learned and infinitely less emancipated from prejudice than those of this country.

THOMAS JEFFERSON TO GEORGE WYTHE,
AUGUST 13, 1786

9

THE QUESTION OF IMMIGRATION

J EFFERSON WAS AN EARLY and strong advocate of the idea that the strength of a nation was in its people. As a result, he welcomed immigrants who were committed to the principles and Constitution of the United States. For example, when he became president, he supported a dramatic reduction in the amount of time necessary before an immigrant could become a citizen. And, as previously noted, he was an early advocate of a broad, free, public education, historically the great engine of assimilation into the nation. Beyond the benefits that immigration offered the nation, Jefferson also called on a free America to be a haven for "oppressed humanity."

> All persons who by their own oath or affirmation,
> or by other testimony shall give satisfactory proof
> to any court of record in this colony that they pur-
> pose to reside in the same [seven] years at the least

and who shall subscribe the fundamental laws, shall be considered as residents and entitled to all the rights of persons natural born.

THOMAS JEFFERSON, THIRD DRAFT,
VIRGINIA CONSTITUTION, JUNE 1776

I cannot omit recommending a revisal of the laws on the subject of naturalization. Considering the ordinary chances of human life, a denial of citizenship, under a residence of fourteen years, is a denial to a great proportion of those who ask it; and controls a policy pursued from their first settlement by many of these states, and still believed of consequence to their prosperity. And shall we refuse to the unhappy fugitives from distress, that hospitality which the savages of the wilderness extended to our fathers arriving in this land? Shall oppressed humanity find no asylum on this globe?

THOMAS JEFFERSON, FIRST ANNUAL
MESSAGE TO CONGRESS,
DECEMBER 8, 1801

A foreigner of any nation, not in open war with us, becomes naturalized by removing to the state to reside, and taking an oath of fidelity: and thereupon acquires every right of a native citizen. . . .

THOMAS JEFFERSON, *NOTES ON THE STATE OF VIRGINIA*,
QUERY XIV

The laws of humanity make it a duty for nations, as well as individuals, to succor those whom accident and distress have thrown upon them.

THOMAS JEFFERSON TO ALBERT GALLATIN,
JANUARY 24, 1807

Monticello, Little Mountain, a place forever known as the beloved home of the man who captured in words, better than anyone before or since, the essence of what makes America special. Why America still draws hopeful people from around the world.

COLIN POWELL, INDEPENDENCE DAY ADDRESS
AT MONTICELLO, JULY 4, 1997

One of the reasons why it is so important for America to continue to welcome new immigrants is not just to maintain our tradition of openness and opportunity but also to remind us of what citizenship really means. Near the end of his life Jefferson wrote that he hoped Americans would use the Fourth of July as a day to "refresh our recollections of [our] rights, and an undiminished devotion to them." I'm afraid we haven't done a very good job of fulfilling that wish. The simple fact—sad but true—is that most of us take our freedoms for granted, and we need you [immigrants] to help us realize how precious they are.

RICHARD MOE, PRESIDENT, NATIONAL TRUST
FOR HISTORIC PRESERVATION, INDEPENDENCE DAY
ADDRESS AT MONTICELLO, JULY 4, 1996

Thomas Jefferson believed that nature has given to all men a right to depart from the country in which chance, not choice, has placed them and to seek "public happiness" in other societies and places where there are more appropriate laws.

VARTAN GREGORIAN, PRESIDENT,
CARNEGIE CORPORATION OF NEW YORK,
INDEPENDENCE DAY ADDRESS AT MONTICELLO,
JULY 4, 2001

Jefferson believed that naturalization was a key to the prosperity and happiness of the people of the newly born United States. He also came to believe that America had an obligation to provide asylum to the oppressed abroad.

JAMES S. GILMORE III, GOVERNOR OF
THE COMMONWEALTH OF VIRGINIA,
INDEPENDENCE DAY ADDRESS AT MONTICELLO,
JULY 4, 1999

Thomas Jefferson and the men who founded the American republic possessed a vision of freedom that mandated an American citizenship open to all who would embrace the concept of liberty and swear allegiance to the constitutional principles of a society whose citizens governed themselves through a system of laws. To deny those "Blessings of Liberty" to any who would seek them here, Jefferson and his colleagues knew, would destroy the very foundation of the free society they sought to create.

CHARLES S. ROBB, GOVERNOR OF
THE COMMONWEALTH OF VIRGINIA,
INDEPENDENCE DAY ADDRESS AT MONTICELLO,
JULY 5, 1982

10

THREATS TO THE REPUBLIC

T HE NATURE OF AMERICA'S open and democratic government came with risks that Jefferson foresaw: Foreign interference in elections, excessive debt, dogmatic demagogues, and politicians focused solely on their own power could undermine the nation and its liberties.

> It becomes of so much consequence to certain nations to have a friend or a foe at the head of our affairs that they will interfere [in an election] with money and with arms.
>
> THOMAS JEFFERSON TO JAMES MADISON,
> DECEMBER 20, 1787

> The care of human life and happiness, and not their destruction, is the first and only legitimate object of good government.
>
> THOMAS JEFFERSON TO THE REPUBLICANS OF
> WASHINGTON COUNTY, MARYLAND, MARCH 31, 1809

I am not among those who fear the people. They, and not the rich, are our dependence for continued freedom. And, to preserve their independence, we must not let our rulers load us with perpetual debt.

THOMAS JEFFERSON TO SAMUEL KERCHEVAL,
JULY 12, 1816

God bless you, and all our rulers, and give them the wisdom, as I am sure they have the will, to fortify us against the degeneracy of our government, and the concentration of all its powers in the hands of the one, the few, the well-born or but the many.

THOMAS JEFFERSON TO JOSEPH C. CABELL,
FEBRUARY 2, 1816

No government has a legitimate right to do what is not for the welfare of the governed.

THOMAS JEFFERSON TO GEORGE WASHINGTON,
SEPTEMBER 9, 1792

We owe gratitude to France, justice to England, good will to all, and subservience to none.

THOMAS JEFFERSON TO ARTHUR CAMPBELL,
SEPTEMBER 1, 1797

Where the law of the majority ceases to be acknowledged, there government ends, the law of the strongest takes its place, and life and property are his who can take them.

THOMAS JEFFERSON TO JOHN GASSAWAY,
FEBRUARY 17, 1809

Ill-tempered and rude men in society who have taken up a passion for politics, . . . from both of these classes of disputants . . . keep aloof, as you would from the infected subjects of yellow fever or pestilence. Consider yourself, when with them, as among the patients of Bedlam needing medical more than moral counsel. Be a listener only, keep within yourself, and endeavor to establish with yourself the habit of silence especially in politics.

In the fevered state of our country, no good can ever result from any attempt to set one of these fiery zealots to rights either in fact or principle. They are determined as to the facts they will believe and the opinions on which they will act. Get by them therefore as you would by an angry bull: It is not for a man of sense to dispute the road with such an animal. . . . Never therefore consider these puppies in politics as requiring any notice from you, and always shew that you are not afraid to leave my character to the umpirage of public opinion.

THOMAS JEFFERSON TO THOMAS JEFFERSON
RANDOLPH, NOVEMBER 24, 1808

11

THE UTILITY OF HOPE

WHILE JEFFERSON LIVED, and governed, through a number of extraordinary crises, and was well aware of threats to the republic, he was fundamentally and emphatically optimistic about the United States, its people, and humanity. If the people insisted on their rights, and exercised their civic responsibilities, all would be well.

He also knew that each generation would face new challenges that its predecessors could not possibly understand, and each generation would have to chart its own course. But if each generation had equal freedom, education, a free press, religious freedom, and a sound government—and actively participated in that government—each generation could succeed and move the nation ever forward.

"I like the dreams of the future better than the history of the past," he famously told John Adams, and confidently concluded "I will dream on. . . ."

The times have been awful, but they have proved an useful truth that the good citizen must never despair of the commonwealth.

THOMAS JEFFERSON TO NATHANIEL NILES,
MARCH 22, 1801

Of all the cankers of human happiness, none corrodes it with so silent, yet so baneful a tooth, as indolence. . . . It is a part of the American character to consider nothing as desperate; to surmount every difficulty by resolution and contrivance. . . .

THOMAS JEFFERSON TO MARTHA JEFFERSON,
MARCH 28, 1787

I shall not die without a hope that light and liberty are on steady advance.

THOMAS JEFFERSON TO JOHN ADAMS,
SEPTEMBER 12, 1821

Possessing ourselves the combined blessings of liberty and order, we wish the same to other countries. . . .

THOMAS JEFFERSON TO ADAMANTIOS KORAÏS,
OCTOBER 31, 1823

Some men look at constitutions with sanctimonious reverence, and deem them, like the ark of the covenant, too sacred to be touched. They ascribe to the men of the preceding age a wisdom more than human, and suppose what they did to be beyond amendment. I knew that age well: I belonged to it, and labored with it. It deserved well of its country. It was very like the present, but without the experience of the present. . . .

THOMAS JEFFERSON TO SAMUEL KERCHEVAL,
JULY 12, 1816

I know also that laws and institutions must go hand in hand with the progress of the human mind. As that becomes more developed, more enlightened, as new discoveries are made, new truths disclosed, and manners and opinions change with the change of circumstances, institutions must advance also, and keep pace with the times.

THOMAS JEFFERSON TO SAMUEL KERCHEVAL,
JULY 12, 1816

We might as well require a man to wear still the coat which fitted him when a boy, as civilized society to remain ever under the regimen of their barbarous ancestors. It is this preposterous idea which has lately deluged Europe in blood. Their monarchs, instead of wisely yielding to the gradual changes of circumstances, of favoring progressive accommodation to progressive improvement, have clung to old abuses, entrenched themselves behind steady habits, and obliged their subjects to seek, thro' blood and violence, rash and ruinous innovations, which, had they been referred to the peaceful deliberations and collected wisdom of the nation, would have been put into acceptable and salutary forms. Let us follow no such examples, nor weakly believe that one generation is not as capable as another of taking care of itself, and of ordering its own affairs.

THOMAS JEFFERSON TO SAMUEL KERCHEVAL,
JULY 12, 1816

A just and solid republican government maintained here, will be a standing monument and example for the aim and imitation of the people of other countries. . . .

THOMAS JEFFERSON TO JOHN DICKINSON,
MARCH 6, 1801

12

PERSPECTIVES ON JEFFERSON

S INCE THE VERY INFANCY of the United States, Thomas Jefferson has spoken for America, for its hopes and dreams, its vision. In the Declaration of Independence, he crafted our mission statement; in the Statute for Religious Freedom, he bespoke America's creed of religious liberty; in his plans for broad, free public education, he understood America's promise. While recognizing some of America's greatest failings, and participating in what he understood to be the loathsome institution of slavery, he also spoke most powerfully to our better nature, to what America could be. Peter Onuf, America's preeminent Jefferson scholar, concluded that "Jefferson—in his visionary moments— seems to know" all Americans. Perhaps better than any other of the Founders, Jefferson expressed not only what America could be, but what we want to be, what we want to believe about ourselves and our nation.

American leaders, political and intellectual, have often, then, reflected on the power of Jefferson's vision.

If our country is to be secure and prosperous in the new century, we must be more than consumers of liberty; we must be the champions and vindicators of it. We must join with others who believe in what Jefferson called the "sacred fire of freedom," and ensure that the democratic tide remains a rising tide around the world.

MADELEINE K. ALBRIGHT, INDEPENDENCE DAY ADDRESS AT MONTICELLO, JULY 4, 2000

An inspiration for the ages, Thomas Jefferson was never satisfied with the status quo. Not in any facet of life. And we are all the beneficiaries of his positive restlessness, his insatiable drive to make things better.

MUHTAR KENT, CHAIRMAN AND CEO, COCA-COLA COMPANY, INDEPENDENCE DAY ADDRESS AT MONTICELLO, JULY 4, 2011

In Jefferson's eyes, . . . science and democracy were connected. . . . He said that it was the light of science that had made it obvious to everyone that, "The mass of mankind has not been [born] with saddles on their backs, the favored few booted and spurred."

CARL SAGAN, INDEPENDENCE DAY ADDRESS AT MONTICELLO, JULY 4, 1992

This place embodies an optimism and confidence in human progress that has existed only rarely in human history. Thomas Jefferson believed in the people with a tenacity that survives in many of our germinal statements about the nature of government and in the institutions he created to protect the people.

JOHN T. CASTEEN III, INDEPENDENCE DAY ADDRESS AT MONTICELLO, JULY 4, 1993

If you want to understand this country and its people and what it means to be optimistic and complex and tragic and wrong and courageous, you need to go to his home in Virginia. Monticello.

MAIRA KALMAN, AUTHOR AND ARTIST, "TIME WASTES TOO FAST," *THE NEW YORK TIMES,* JUNE 25, 2009

[Jefferson] not only knew the literature and the science, but the other great thing which is the secret of a free society, and that is a rule of law.

MARGARET THATCHER, FORMER BRITISH PRIME MINISTER, APRIL 13, 1996

This stern man, such a strong person of principle, yet understood the weakness of human nature, especially in times of difficulty, and said, "please understand [in his inaugural address]." The person who said that will also understand the difficulties of others.

MARGARET THATCHER, APRIL 13, 1996

13

OTHER PRESIDENTS ON JEFFERSON AND JEFFERSONIAN AMERICA

T HROUGHOUT AMERICAN HISTORY, other presidents have recognized the foundational role that Jefferson's vision played both in the formation of the republic and in maintaining the rights and responsibilities of citizens. Seeing the operation of the nation from the pinnacle of government power, they have over and over again called on Jefferson, and called on all of us to protect a Jeffersonian republic.

He lives and will live in the memory and gratitude of the wise and good, as a luminary of science, as a votary of liberty, as a model of patriotism, and as a benefactor of human kind.

JAMES MADISON TO NICHOLAS P. TRIST,
JULY 6, 1826

This Act [Jefferson's Statute for Establishing Religious Freedom] is a true standard of religious liberty:

its principle the great *barrier ag[ain]st usurpations on the rights of conscience. As long as it is respected* and no longer, *these will be safe. Every provision for them—short of this principle, will be found to leave crevices at least, thro' which bigotry may introduce persecution; a monster, that feeding and thriving on its own venom, gradually swells to a size and strength overwhelming all laws divine and human. Ye States of America which retain in your constitutions or codes any aberration from the sacred principle of religious liberty, by giving to Caesar what belongs to God, or joining together what God has put asunder, hasten to revise your systems, and make the example of your country as pure and compleat, in what relates to the freedom of the mind and its allegiance to its maker, as in what belongs to the legitimate objects of political and civil institutions.*

JAMES MADISON, DETACHED MEMORANDUM,
CA. JANUARY 31, 1820

The principles of Jefferson are the definitions and axioms of free society. . . . Those who deny freedom to others, deserve it not for themselves; and, under a just God, cannot long retain it. All honor to Jefferson—to the man who, in the concrete pressure of a struggle for national independence by a single people, had the coolness, forecast, and capacity to introduce into a merely revolutionary document, an abstract truth, and so to embalm it there, that today and in all coming days, it shall be a rebuke and a stumbling-block to the very harbingers of reappearing tyranny and oppression.

ABRAHAM LINCOLN TO HENRY L. PIERCE ET AL., APRIL 6, 1859

Jefferson's principles are sources of light because they are not made up of pure reason, but spring out of aspiration, impulse, vision, sympathy. They burn with the fervor of the heart.

WOODROW WILSON, 1912

Monopoly, private control, the authority of privilege, the concealed mastery of a few men ... [Thomas Jefferson] would have moved against them, sometimes directly, sometimes indirectly, sometimes openly, sometimes subtly; but whether he merely mined about them, or struck directly at them, he would have set systematic war against them at the front of all his purpose.

As regards the economic policy of the country it is perfectly plain that Mr. Jefferson would have insisted upon a tariff fitted to actual conditions, by which he would have meant not the interests of the few men who find access to the hearings of the Ways and Means Committee of the House and the Finance Committee of the Senate, but the interests of the business men and manufacturers and farmers and workers and professional men of every kind and class. . . .

In the general field of business his thought would, of course, have gone about to establish freedom, to throw business opportunities open at every point to new men, to destroy the processes of monopoly, to exclude the poison of special favors, to see that, whether big or little, business was not dominated by anything but the law itself.

WOODROW WILSON, JEFFERSON DINNER ADDRESS,
APRIL 14, 1912

The immortality of Thomas Jefferson does not lie in any one of his achievements, or in the series of his achievements, but in his attitude towards mankind and the conception which he sought to realize in action of the service owed by America to the rest of the world. . . . It is not a circumstance without significance that Jefferson felt, perhaps more than any other American of his time, except Benjamin Franklin, his close kinship with like thinking spirits everywhere else in the civilized world. . . . If you are ready, you have inherited the spirit of Jefferson, who recognized the men in France and the men in Germany who were doing the liberal thinking of their day as just as much citizens of the great work of liberty as he was himself, and who was ready in every conception he had to join hands across the water or across any other barrier with those who held those high conceptions of liberty which had brought the United States into existence.

WOODROW WILSON, JEFFERSON DAY ADDRESS,
APRIL 13, 1916

Constantly he labored to enlarge the freedom of the human mind, to destroy the bondage imposed on it by ignorance, poverty, and political and religious intolerance.

FRANKLIN D. ROOSEVELT, INDEPENDENCE DAY
ADDRESS AT MONTICELLO, JULY 4, 1936

And so, through all the intervening years, America has lived and grown under the system of government established by Jefferson and his generation. . . . The honors which other men have given him are unimportant. The opportunities he had given to other men to become free were all that really counted.

FRANKLIN D. ROOSEVELT, INDEPENDENCE DAY
ADDRESS AT MONTICELLO, JULY 4, 1936

He applied the culture of the past to the needs and the life of the America of his day. His knowledge of history spurred him to inquire into the reason and the justice of laws and habits and institutions. His passion for liberty led him to interpret and adapt in order to better the lot of mankind.

FRANKLIN D. ROOSEVELT, INDEPENDENCE DAY
ADDRESS AT MONTICELLO, JULY 4, 1936

It was the purpose of Jefferson to teach the country that the solidarity of Federalism was only a partial one, that it represented only a minority of the people, that to build a great Nation the interests of all groups in every part must be considered, and that only in a large, national unity could real security be found.

FRANKLIN D. ROOSEVELT,
JEFFERSON DAY DINNER ADDRESS,
APRIL 18, 1932

Thomas Jefferson is a hero to me . . . because, in his many-sided genius, he too did the big job that then had to be done—to establish the new republic as a real democracy based on universal suffrage and the in-alienable rights of man, instead of a restricted suffrage in the hands of a small oligarchy. Jefferson realized that if the people were free to get and discuss all the facts, their composite judgment would be better than the judgment of a self-perpetuating few. That is why I think of Jefferson as belonging to the rank and file of both major political parties today.

FRANKLIN D. ROOSEVELT,
JACKSON DAY DINNER ADDRESS,
JANUARY 8, 1940

I have profound faith in the people of this country. I believe in their common sense. They love freedom, and that love for freedom and justice is not dead. Our people believe today, as Jefferson did, that men were not born with saddles on their backs to be ridden by the privileged few.

HARRY S. TRUMAN, SEPTEMBER 27, 1948

To reach the summit of our hopes it is the human lot, regardless of disappointments and fatigue, to disdain the plateaus of ease and the downward slopes of complacency, for we have learned from ages past that these, in spite of their enticing foreground, dead-end, inevitably, in despair and anguish.

Yet, to many among us in these times, the plateaus and slopes seem to have an irresistible appeal.

Viewed in this perspective, the developing posture of our country cannot comfort any thoughtful person, in or out of government.

In pondering the reasons for this modern trend, my mind goes back to almost two centuries ago, when a youthful colonist, destined for immortality, took up his pen to define his concept of the inalienable rights of free men.

In the golden words of Thomas Jefferson, these rights included "life, liberty and the pursuit of happiness."

It is clear, I believe, that he was one who did not equate happiness with affluence, self-indulgence, or idleness; but we wonder, whether in some modern misinterpretation of this revered phrase—known to every generation of Americans from childhood—is to be found the origin of some of our anxieties today.

Had Jefferson foreseen any possibility that "pursuit of happiness" might one day be read as justifying self-ish and empty purposes, I suspect he would have, at the very least, added a footnote of explanation, if not of caution, for our current benefit.

DWIGHT D. EISENHOWER,
GOVERNORS' CONFERENCE,
JUNE 8, 1964

To Thomas Jefferson, author of the Declaration, is at-tributed this statement: "The whole of government is the art of honesty." The cynics may brush off that statement, too, with the tag, "Platitude." But out of my half century in the service of our nation I would say Thomas Jefferson compressed into those nine words a truth about Government that lesser men could not so sharply define in a lengthy campaign of speeches or a year's production of press releases.

DWIGHT D. EISENHOWER,
OCTOBER 10, 1964

"The freedom and happiness of man," said Thomas Jef-ferson, "are the sole objects of all legitimate govern-ment." This quotation of Jefferson . . . is the alpha and omega of our existence, and as long as it is followed, America will be free and secure. . . . Jefferson advocated a wide extension of suffrage and the fullest measure of personal liberty of speech, of religion, and the press, in

keeping with the maintenance of law, order, and the overall national welfare.

> JOHN F. KENNEDY, DEMOCRATIC PARTY
> JEFFERSON DINNER,
> JUNE 3, 1947

We are not lulled by the momentary calm of the sea or the somewhat clearer skies above. We know the turbulence that lies below, and the storms that are beyond the horizons this year. But now the winds of change appear to be blowing more strongly than ever. . . . For 175 years we have sailed with those winds at our back, and with the tides of human freedom in our favor. We steer our ship with hope, as Thomas Jefferson said, "leaving fear astern."

> JOHN F. KENNEDY, STATE OF THE UNION MESSAGE,
> JANUARY 14, 1963

I ask all Americans, in their homes, their schools, and their places of work, to reflect on the life and times of Thomas Jefferson. I urge every American to reflect on the meaning and purpose of the Declaration of Independence and the many other works of Thomas Jefferson. . . .

> GERALD R. FORD, THOMAS JEFFERSON DAY
> PROCLAMATION, APRIL 13, 1976

"Men may be trusted," he said, "to govern themselves without a master." This was the most revolutionary

*idea in the world at the time. It remains the most revo-
lutionary idea in the world today.*

GERALD R. FORD, INDEPENDENCE DAY ADDRESS
AT MONTICELLO, JULY 5, 1976

*Thomas Jefferson conceived our United States of Amer-
ica as no other nation had ever tried to be—dedicated to
human fulfillment, where individual liberty was guar-
anteed. But Thomas Jefferson also founded a university, collected a national library, planned beautiful
cities, mapped the wilderness, and, being a farmer, he
invented a better plow!*

JIMMY CARTER, NATIONAL DEMOCRATIC PARTY
CONFERENCE, DECEMBER 8, 1978

*The pursuit of science, the study of the great works, the
value of free inquiry, in short, the very idea of living
the life of the mind—yes, these formative and abiding
principles of higher education in America had their
first and firmest advocate, and their great embodiment,
in a tall, fair-headed, friendly man who watched this
university [UVA] take form from the mountainside
where he lived, the university whose founding he
called a crowning achievement to a long and well-
spent life.*

RONALD REAGAN, REMARKS AT THE
UNIVERSITY OF VIRGINIA IN CHARLOTTESVILLE,
DECEMBER 16, 1988

It's not just students and presidents, it is every American—indeed, every human life ever touched by the daring idea of self-government—that Mr. Jefferson has influenced.

RONALD REAGAN, REMARKS AT THE
UNIVERSITY OF VIRGINIA IN CHARLOTTESVILLE,
DECEMBER 16, 1988

He knew how disorderly a place the world could be. Indeed, as a leader of a rebellion, he was himself an architect, if you will, of disorder. But he also believed that man had received from God a precious gift of enlightenment—the gift of reason, a gift that could extract from the chaos of life meaning, truth, order.

RONALD REAGAN, REMARKS AT THE
UNIVERSITY OF VIRGINIA IN CHARLOTTESVILLE,
DECEMBER 16, 1988

Our children are also the beneficiaries of a nation that lavishes unsurpassed resources on their schooling. So, in many ways we're close to fulfilling the Enlightenment dream of universal education, a dream that became a reality in the shadows of the Shenandoahs here at Mr. Jefferson's school.

And every step we take at this university is truly a walk in Thomas Jefferson's footsteps. . . .

We have already come close to this Jeffersonian ideal. Our educational system is, in many ways, unrivaled in its scale and its diversity, in its commitment to meeting special needs and individual differences. And we're inspired by our best teachers, who give more than we can rightly expect, and from our best students, who surpass our highest expectations. And yet, after two centuries of progress, we are stagnant. While millions of Americans read for pleasure, millions of others don't read at all. And while millions go to college, millions may never graduate from high school.

GEORGE H. W. BUSH, REMARKS AT THE
UNIVERSITY OF VIRGINIA CONVOCATION
IN CHARLOTTESVILLE, SEPTEMBER 28, 1989

Thomas Jefferson was one of our greatest presidents and perhaps our most brilliant president. . . . He believed in the power of ideas which have made this country great. . . . Jefferson believed in public service.

BILL CLINTON, KICKOFF OF INAUGURAL JOURNEY
AT MONTICELLO, JANUARY 17, 1993

Thomas Jefferson believed that to preserve the very foundations of our nation, we would need dramatic change from time to time. Well, my fellow citizens, this is our time. Let us embrace it.

BILL CLINTON, FIRST INAUGURAL ADDRESS,
JANUARY 21, 1993

The principles that Thomas Jefferson enshrined in the Declaration became the guiding principles of the new nation. And at every generation, Americans have re-

dedicated themselves to the belief that all men are created equal, with the God-given right to life, liberty, and the pursuit of happiness.

GEORGE W. BUSH, INDEPENDENCE DAY ADDRESS
AT MONTICELLO, JULY 4, 2008

As one of our Founding Fathers, the person who drafted our Declaration of Independence, somebody who not only was an extraordinary political leader but also one of our great scientific and cultural leaders, Thomas Jefferson represents what's best in America.

BARACK OBAMA, REMARKS AFTER TOURING
THOMAS JEFFERSON'S MONTICELLO,
FEBRUARY 10, 2014

Afterword

ANNETTE GORDON-REED

In the fall of 2012, seventeen years after my first visit to Monticello, and fifteen years after I had published my first book about Jefferson, I finally made it to the Jefferson Memorial, situated, somewhat inconveniently, at a distance from the other Washington, D.C., monuments. I had passed it many times on the way to and from Reagan National Airport; each time peering out the window to catch a glimpse of the towering statue that flickered between the rows of columns supporting that familiar dome—a larger-than-life Jefferson encased in a building reminiscent of his two great architectural passions, Monticello and the University of Virginia—right there on the banks of the Tidal Basin.

It was something else again to go inside the structure and see Rudulph Evans's nineteen-and-a-half-foot bronze statue in the midst of interior walls that reproduce Jefferson's famous words. The juxtaposition is fitting, for words and writing were so central to the role he played as a revolutionary and politician in the early American republic. Words, and the feelings they inspired, made Jefferson who he was. "The pen of the Revolution" wrote words that moved his generation, and those that followed, in the United States and across the globe: *We hold these truths to be self-evident that all men are created equal, that they are endowed by their Creator with certain unalienable Rights, that among these are Life, Liberty and the pursuit of Happiness.*

I knew even before I arrived that other of Jefferson's words would be missing—the ones where he cast doubt on the capacity of forming a multiracial society in the country he helped to create. With those words, Jefferson was mostly a product of his time and place—a white Virginian of the eighteenth century. His prodigious imagination allowed him to see many things but did not allow him to take in the possibility that whites would be able give up their prejudices and live in harmony with blacks as equal citizens in a republican society. For as much as we condemn those words, it would be fantasy to pretend that Jefferson did not have good cause to question this possibility. He did not become the most successful politician of his age without understanding the mood and attitudes of the majority of white society, whose favor he sought and on whom his success depended.

Even after a civil war that ended slavery, and the

amendment of the Constitution in the postwar years to bring blacks into citizenship, it has been a constant struggle for the intent of those amendments to be realized. One hundred and ninety-four years after Jefferson's death, it is still too soon to declare complete victory on that front. Ironically, this has been a struggle in which Jefferson's words about the equality of all mankind have played a perennial and central role. Every major black leader has made use of them in the fight for true black citizenship. Early on, the declaration gave ammunition to blacks in the Revolutionary period and the early American republic who sought to end slavery and create a better life for African Americans. Indeed, as the years have passed, *every* group that has sought equality in the United States—women, religious minorities, immigrants—has relied on Jefferson's words to make the case for inclusion.

My head filled with impressions from this first encounter with the memorial, I decided upon leaving that a long walk was in order. Deep in thought, walking along the path leading away from the monument, I suddenly heard footsteps coming fast behind me. I assumed they had nothing to do with me until my peripheral vision brought a young woman in a National Park Service uniform into view. She stopped running just by my side, turned to me and said, "You're Annette Gordon-Reed." I acknowledged that I was. She said she had seen me walking around the memorial and had intended to talk to me, but I had managed to slip away before she got the chance. Still nearly breathless, she told me she had read all I had written about Jefferson, and wanted to talk to me about him, and tell me why she thought he was an important figure, and how he had come to mean something in her life.

The words poured out. She had arrived in the United States as a preteen from Somalia and had soon become interested in Jefferson after reading about him and the Declaration of Independence. She felt compelled to read more, and what sold her on him completely was what he had to say about the separation of church and state and the importance of science and progress. She offered that Americans did not sufficiently appreciate the benefits of living in a society in which the government proclaimed no religious orthodoxy—indeed one in which a respected Founder had taken a position against such an orthodoxy so clearly and steadfastly. And the idea of progress, of human beings improving themselves with effort and education, was enormously appealing to her. Her family had left Somalia (the country, for most of her childhood, in a near anarchic state) because they did not believe such improvement was possible there.

I was more than a little taken aback in the face of this totally unabashed hero worship coming from this particular source. A young female African immigrant, now citizen of the United States and Thomas Jefferson enthusiast, was not at all who I expected to encounter when I decided to make my first foray to the Jefferson Memorial. Unlike many people I talk to about Jefferson, this young woman had read a good deal of what he had written. Her judgment was considered. Still, I raised the obvious and difficult questions: What about slavery? What about race? "Oh, I know all about that," she said with the wave of a hand. Everyone has flaws. But in this case, as far as she was concerned, the flaws did not outweigh his contributions or the importance of his more admirable ideas. I pressed a bit harder on the point. But she was unfazed. Americans, she said firmly, fixate too much on the person and not the ideas.

For her, Jefferson was about the ideas, the words that voiced truths that had staying power across the ages and geography. I could only think that her family's experiences in the land of her birth had shaped her attitude toward one who, despite very human lapses, believed in the power of reason to help shape an ordered society and put in place a governmental system that would work on behalf of all citizens. Who knows what our third president would think of the conversation about him that took place in the shadow of his monument. He might see it as evidence that his hope for the declaration, expressed in his letter to Roger Chew

Weightman written in the month before he died, might actually be coming true: "May it be to the world, what I believe it will be, (to some parts sooner, to others later, but finally to all)." I know one young Somali American thinks so.

Sources

The letters of Thomas Jefferson as well as the Rockfish Gap Report, the Bill for the More General Diffusion of Knowledge, the Virginia Statute for Religious Freedom, and Jefferson's essay commonly referred to as his *Autobiography* can be found in *The Papers of Thomas Jefferson,* edited by Julian P. Boyd et al., 44 vols. to date (Princeton, N.J.: Princeton University Press, 1950–); *The Papers of Thomas Jefferson, Retirement Series,* edited by J. Jefferson Looney et al., 16 vols. to date (Princeton, N.J.: Princeton University Press, 2004–); and *Founders Online,* National Archives, https://www.founders.archives.gov/. Jefferson's *Notes on the State of Virginia* are edited by William Peden (Chapel Hill: University of North Carolina Press, 1982). Other materials are quoted from publicly available sources.

ADDITIONAL READING

Cogliano, Francis D., ed. *A Companion to Thomas Jefferson.* Malden, Mass.: Wiley-Blackwell, 2011.

Gordon-Reed, Annette, and Peter Onuf. *"Most Blessed of the Patriarchs": Thomas Jefferson and the Empire of the Imagination.* New York: Liveright, 2017.

Meacham, Jon. *Thomas Jefferson: The Art of Power.* New York: Random House, 2012.

ABOUT THE AUTHORS

JON MEACHAM is the author of numerous *New York Times* bestsellers, including the Pulitzer Prize–winning biography *American Lion: Andrew Jackson in the White House*. He holds the Carolyn T. and Robert M. Rogers Chair in the American Presidency and is a distinguished visiting professor at Vanderbilt University. A trustee of the Thomas Jefferson Foundation at Monticello and a fellow of the Society of American Historians, Meacham lives in Nashville.

ANNETTE GORDON-REED is the Charles Warren Professor of American Legal History at Harvard Law School and a professor of history in the Faculty of Arts and Sciences at Harvard University. She was awarded the Pulitzer Prize for History and the National Book Award for Nonfiction for her work on the Hemings family of Monticello, where she serves as a trustee. She lives in New York City and Cambridge, Massachusetts.

JOHN A. RAGOSTA is the Joseph and Robert Cornell Memorial Foundation Senior Historian at the Robert H. Smith International Center for Jefferson Studies at Monticello and has taught law and history at the University of Virginia, George Washington University, and Oberlin, Hamilton, and Randolph Colleges.

ABOUT THE TYPES

This book was set in Requiem, a typeface designed by the Hoefler Type Foundry. It is a modern typeface inspired by inscriptional capitals in Ludovico Vicentino degli Arrighi's 1523 writing manual, *Il modo de temperare le penne*. An original lowercase, a set of figures, and an italic in the chancery style that Arrighi (fl. 1522) helped popularize were created to make this adaptation of a classical design into a complete font family.

This book was also set in Nofret, a typeface designed in 1986 by Gudrun Zapf-von Hesse especially for the Berthold foundry.